CALM
THE
F*CK
DOWN

AN IRREVERENT BOOK OF SH*T YOU NEED TO LET GO

S sourcebooks

Calm the
fuck down.

You listen to podcasts?

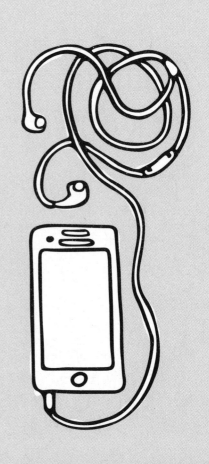

Calm the
fuck down.

Oh, you "Kondo'd"
your closet...

Calm the fuck down.

You *ran* a marathon?

Calm the
fuck down.

FINISH

We had to censor the cover of this book...

Your team won.

Calm the
fuck down.

Your team lost.

Calm the
fuck down.

You don't like sports.

Calm the
fuck down.

You brew your
own beer.

Calm the fuck down.

You forgot to take the Instagram photo before you ate?

Calm the fuck down.

Oh, *your* family is dysfunctional?

Calm the
fuck down.

You love **dogs**
more than **people**.

Calm the fuck down.

Rosé all day.

Calm the
fuck down.

Oh no! Someone didn't use their turn signal!

Calm the
fuck down.

Millennials...

Calm the
fuck down.

Someone said

Calm the

FUCK

down.

Snapchat filters...

Calm the fuck down.
You look better as
a puppy.

March Madness.

Calm the
fuck down.

You play guitar?

Calm the
fuck down.

Unicorns.

Calm the
fuck down.

You "hygge."

Calm the
fuck down.

You know what
"hygge" is?

Calm the
fuck down.

Your baby is *not* that cute.

Calm the
fuck down.

Calm the
fuck down.

Yes, Trump got elected.

Calm the
fuck down.

"They" is an acceptable singular pronoun.

Calm the
fuck down.

You're offended by one
of the last two pages...

Calm the
fuck down.

The book is *always* better than the movie.

Calm the
fuck down.

Your cat is a genius?

Calm the
fuck down.

You're on a "cleanse."

Calm the
fuck down.

Face it. You're not going to live on Mars in your lifetime.

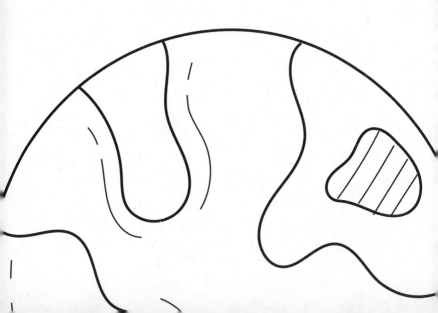

(Or any other damn planet but Earth.
Start recycling, bitch.)

You own an Alexa but you're upset when she listens to you?

Calm the
fuck down.

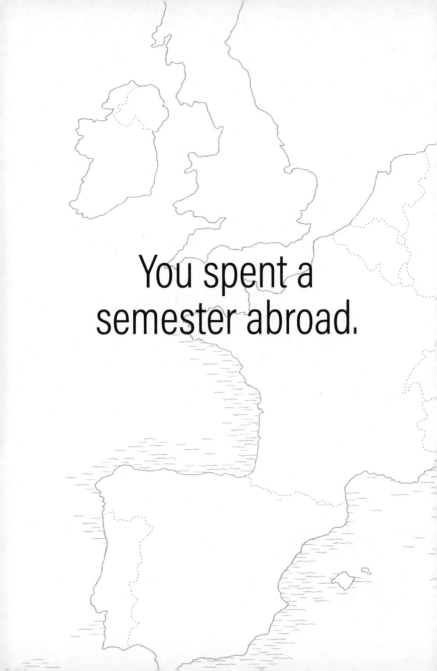

You spent a
semester abroad.

Calm the
fuck down.

"Fake news."

Calm the
fuck down.

The royal family.

Calm the fuck down.

You use the word "adulting."

Calm the
fuck down.

You like knitting.

Calm. The.
Fuck. Down.

Daylight Savings.

Calm the fuck down and take a nap.

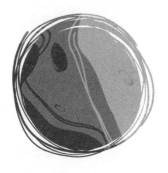

Mercury is in retrograde?

Calm the fuck down.

You eat quinuoa...
quinua...queenoa.

Calm the
fuck down.

FUCKING QUINOA.

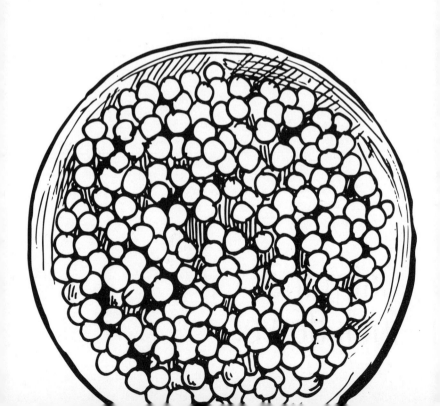

Calm the
fuck down.

Somebody called you instead of texting.

Calm the fuck down.
It's a phone.
It's supposed to ring.

You shop at Whole Foods and spend way too much money.

Calm the
fuck down.

I'm sending thoughts
and prayers!

Calm the
fuck down.

Commercials during the Super Bowl.

Calm the
fuck down.

You call yourself an "influencer."

Calm the fuck down.

You have a tattoo.

Calm the
fuck down.

Artificial Intelligence is *not* taking your job.

Calm the
fuck down.

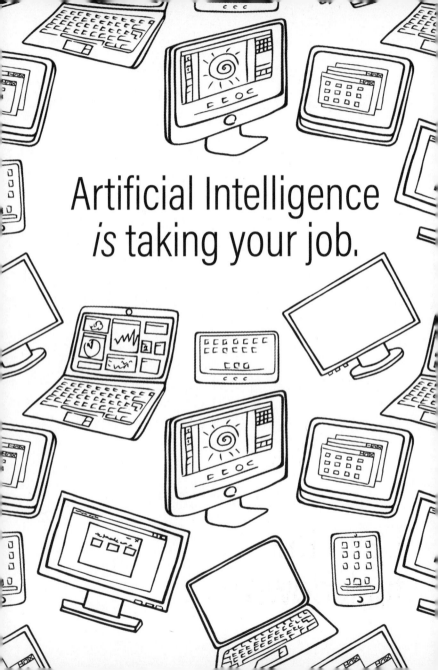

Artificial Intelligence *is* taking your job.

We're sorry.

You're

WO

Calm the
fuck down.

Oh, I'm sorry.
You're gluten free?

Calm the fuck down
and have a salad.

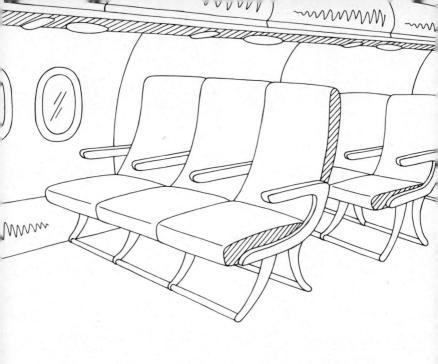

So you got the middle
seat on the plane.

Calm the fuck down.

Your favorite book is *Ulysses*. *eye roll*

Calm the
fuck down.

You own an
Instant Pot?

Calm the
fuck down.

Someone is chewing loudly.

Calm the
fuck down.

You listen to NPR.

Calm the
fuck down.

You voted.

Calm the
fuck down.

We're all becoming robots!!!!

Calm the
fuck down!!!!

You've been to
the happiest place
in the world?

Calm the
fuck down.

You've never been to the happiest place in the world?

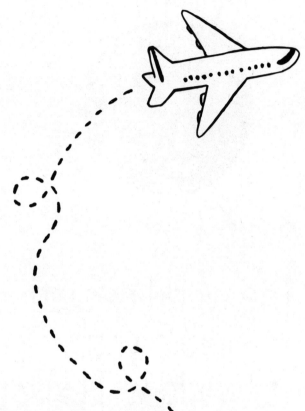

Dammit, book a flight and get your ass over there!

The world existed
before you.
The world will exist
after you.

Calm the
fuck down.

And if you're still upset, here are additional pages where you can calm the fuck down:

_____

_____

_____

_____

_____

_____

_____

_____

_____

_____

_____

_____

_____

_____

_____

_____

_____

_____

_____